Layers of Learning

Year One • Unit Sixteen

Ancient South America
South America
Plants
South American Art

HooDoo Publishing
United States of America

ISBN 978-1495249488

Units At A Glance: Topics For All Four Years of the Layers of Learning Program

1	History	Geography	Science	The Arts
1	Mesopotamia	Maps & Globes	Planets	Cave Paintings
2	Egypt	Map Keys	Stars	Egyptian Art
3	Europe	Global Grids	Earth & Moon	Crafts
4	Ancient Greece	Wonders	Satellites	Greek Art
5	Babylon	Mapping People	Humans in Space	Poetry
6	The Levant	Physical Earth	Laws of Motion	List Poems
7	Phoenicians	Oceans	Motion	Moral Stories
8	Assyrians	Deserts	Fluids	Rhythm
9	Persians	Arctic	Waves	Melody
10	Ancient China	Forests	Machines	Chinese Art
11	Early Japan	Mountains	States of Matter	Line & Shape
12	Arabia	Rivers & Lakes	Atoms	Color & Value
13	Ancient India	Grasslands	Elements	Texture & Form
14	Ancient Africa	Africa	Bonding	African Tales
15	First North Americans	North America	Salts	Creative Kids
16	Ancient South America	South America	Plants	South American Art
17	Celts	Europe	Flowering Plants	Jewelry
18	Roman Republic	Asia	Trees	Roman Art
19	Christianity	Australia & Oceania	Simple Plants	Instruments
20	Roman Empire	You Explore	Fungi	Composing Music

2	History	Geography	Science	The Arts
1	Byzantines	Turkey	Climate & Seasons	Byzantine Art
2	Barbarians	Ireland	Forecasting	Illumination
3	Islam	Arabian Peninsula	Clouds & Precipitation	Creative Kids
4	Vikings	Norway	Special Effects	Viking Art
5	Anglo Saxons	Britain	Wild Weather	King Arthur Tales
6	Charlemagne	France	Cells and DNA	Carolingian Art
7	Normans	Nigeria	Skeletons	Canterbury Tales
8	Feudal System	Germany	Muscles, Skin, & Cardiopulmonary	Gothic Art
9	Crusades	Balkans	Digestive & Senses	Religious Art
10	Burgundy, Venice, Spain	Switzerland	Nerves	Oil Paints
11	Wars of the Roses	Russia	Health	Minstrels & Plays
12	Eastern Europe	Hungary	Metals	Printmaking
13	African Kingdoms	Mali	Carbon Chem	Textiles
14	Asian Kingdoms	Southeast Asia	Non-metals	Vivid Language
15	Mongols	Caucasus	Gases	Fun With Poetry
16	Medieval China & Japan	China	Electricity	Asian Arts
17	Pacific Peoples	Micronesia	Circuits	Arts of the Islands
18	American Peoples	Canada	Technology	Indian Legends
19	The Renaissance	Italy	Magnetism	Renaissance Art I
20	Explorers	Caribbean Sea	Motors	Renaissance Art II

3	History	Geography	Science	The Arts
1	Age of Exploration	Argentina and Chile	Classification & Insects	Fairy Tales
2	The Ottoman Empire	Egypt and Libya	Reptiles & Amphibians	Poetry
3	Mogul Empire	Pakistan & Afghanistan	Fish	Mogul Arts
4	Reformation	Angola & Zambia	Birds	Reformation Art
5	Renaissance England	Tanzania & Kenya	Mammals & Primates	Shakespeare
6	Thirty Years' War	Spain	Sound	Baroque Music
7	The Dutch	Netherlands	Light & Optics	Baroque Art I
8	France	Indonesia	Bending Light	Baroque Art II
9	The Enlightenment	Korean Pen.	Color	Art Journaling
10	Russia & Prussia	Central Asia	History of Science	Watercolors
11	Conquistadors	Baltic States	Igneous Rocks	Creative Kids
12	Settlers	Peru & Bolivia	Sedimentary Rocks	Native American Art
13	13 Colonies	Central America	Metamorphic Rocks	Settler Sayings
14	Slave Trade	Brazil	Gems & Minerals	Colonial Art
15	The South Pacific	Australasia	Fossils	Principles of Art
16	The British in India	India	Chemical Reactions	Classical Music
17	Boston Tea Party	Japan	Reversible Reactions	Folk Music
18	Founding Fathers	Iran	Compounds & Solutions	Rococo
19	Declaring Independence	Samoa and Tonga	Oxidation & Reduction	Creative Crafts I
20	The American Revolution	South Africa	Acids & Bases	Creative Crafts II

4	History	Geography	Science	The Arts
1	American Government	USA	Heat & Temperature	Patriotic Music
2	Expanding Nation	Pacific States	Motors & Engines	Tall Tales
3	Industrial Revolution	U.S. Landscapes	Energy	Romantic Art I
4	Revolutions	Mountain West States	Energy Sources	Romantic Art II
5	Africa	U.S. Political Maps	Energy Conversion	Impressionism I
6	The West	Southwest States	Earth Structure	Impressionism II
7	Civil War	National Parks	Plate Tectonics	Post-Impressionism
8	World War I	Plains States	Earthquakes	Expressionism
9	Totalitarianism	U.S. Economics	Volcanoes	Abstract Art
10	Great Depression	Heartland States	Mountain Building	Kinds of Art
11	World War II	Symbols and Landmarks	Chemistry of Air & Water	War Art
12	Modern East Asia	The South States	Food Chemistry	Modern Art
13	India's Independence	People of America	Industry	Pop Art
14	Israel	Appalachian States	Chemistry of Farming	Modern Music
15	Cold War	U.S. Territories	Chemistry of Medicine	Free Verse
16	Vietnam War	Atlantic States	Food Chains	Photography
17	Latin America	New England States	Animal Groups	Latin American Art
18	Civil Rights	Home State Study	Instincts	Theater & Film
19	Technology	Home State Study II	Habitats	Architecture
20	Terrorism	America in Review	Conservation	Creative Kids

This unit includes printables at the end. To make life easier for you we also created digital printable packs for each unit. To retrieve your printable pack for Unit 1-16, please visit

www.layers-of-learning.com/digital-printable-packs/

Put the printable pack in your shopping cart and use this coupon code:

0117UNIT1-16

Your printable pack will be free.

Layers of Learning Introduction

This is part of a series of units in the Layers of Learning homeschool curriculum, including the subjects of history, geography, science, and the arts. Children from 1st through 12th can participate in the same curriculum at the same time – family school style.

The units are intended to be used in order as the basis of a complete curriculum (once you add in a systematic math, reading, and writing program). You begin with Year 1 Unit 1 no matter what ages your children are. Spend about 2 weeks on each unit. You pick and choose the activities within the unit that appeal to you and read the books from the book list that are available to you or find others on the same topic from your library. We highly recommend that you use the timeline in every history section as the backbone. Then flesh out your learning with reading and activities that highlight the topics you think are the most important.

Alternatively, you can use the units as activity ideas to supplement another curriculum in any order you wish. You can still use them with all ages of children at the same time.

When you've finished with Year One, move on to Year Two, Year Three, and Year Four. Then begin again with Year One and work your way through the years again. Now your children will be older, reading more involved books, and writing more in depth. When you have completed the sequence for the second time, you start again on it for the third and final time. If your student began with Layers of Learning in 1st grade and stayed with it all the way through she would go through the four year rotation three times, firmly cementing the information in her mind in ever increasing depth. At each level you should expect increasing amounts of outside reading and writing. High schoolers in particular should be reading extensively, and if possible, participating in discussion groups.

☻ ☻ ☻ These icons will guide you in spotting activities and books that are appropriate for the age of child you are working with. But if you think an activity is too juvenile or too difficult for your kids, adjust accordingly. The icons are not there as rules, just guides.

☻ Grades 1-4
☻ Grades 5-8
☻ Grades 9-12

Within each unit we share:

- EXPLORATIONS, activities relating to the topic;
- EXPERIMENTS, usually associated with science topics;
- EXPEDITIONS, field trips;
- EXPLANATIONS, teacher helps or educational philosophies.

In the sidebars we also include Additional Layers, Famous Folks, Fabulous Facts, On the Web, and other extra related topics that can take you off on tangents, exploring the world and your interests with a bit more freedom. The curriculum will always be there to pull you back on track when you're ready.

You can learn more about how to use this curriculum at www.layers-of-learning.com/layers-of-learning-program/

Unit Sixteen

Ancient South America – South America – Plants – S. American Art

Listen to the musn'ts, child. Listen to the don'ts. Listen to the shouldn'ts, the impossibles, the won'ts, then listen close to me . . . Anything can happen child. Anything can be.
-Shel Silverstein

	Library List:
History	Search For: ancient South America, Norte Chico, ancient Peru, Chavin, Moche, Canari, Chibchas, ancient Amazon. This is a hard to find topic! ☻ ☻ ☻ National Geographic: http://news.nationalgeographic.com/news/2010/01/100104-amazon-lost-civilization-circles.html Search National Geographic for more on ancient South America. ☻ Jabuti the Tortoise: a Trickster Tale From the Amazon by Gerald McDermott. ☻ The Ancient American World by William Fash and Mary E. Lyons. Several of the chapters cover ancient South America, as well as the Maya and Inca peoples. ☻ Mummies by Christopher Sloan. A cross culture and time look at mummies, ancient and modern, including the people of the Andes. ☻ A Sacred Landscape: The Search For Ancient Peru by Hugh Thompson. The landscape and the history of the people from ancient times. Warning: Contains descriptions of sexually explicit ancient pottery and the author's alcohol use. ☻ Chavin and the Origins of the Andean Civilization by Richard L. Burger.
Geography	Search For: South America ☻ ☻ ☻ CD's of music from South America: samba, tango, and cumbia. ☻ Explore South America by Bobbie Kalman. ☻ ☻ This Place is High by Vikki Cobb. What is it like to live in the Andes Mountains? ☻ ☻ This Place is Wet by Vikki Cobb. What is it like to live in the Amazon Rain Forest? ☻ ☻ South America by Libby Koponen. ☻ In the Land of the Jaguar by Gena K. Gorrell. ☻ Viva South America! By Oliver Balch. A London reporter quits his job, moves to South America, and sets out on a quest to figure out what makes this continent tick.

Science	Search For: plants, plant cells, plant classification, gardening ☻ ☻ Roots, Shoots, Buckets, and Boots by Sharon Lovejoy. Activities to do with kids in the garden. ☻ ☻ Kids Container Gardening by Cindy Krezel. Indoors and outdoors year round projects even if you don't have a back yard. ☻ ☻ Plant Classification by Louise and Richard Spilsbury. ☻ From Seed to Plant by Allan Fowler. A very simple introduction to plants for the youngest students. ☻ The Tiny Seed by Eric Carle. Comes with a seed embedded paper you can plant. ☻ From Seed to Plant by Gail Gibbons. ☻ How a Seed Grows by Helene J. Jordan. ☻ Planting a Rainbow by Lois Ehlert. See also Growing Vegetable Soup by Ehlert. ☻ ☻ Shanleya's Quest: A Botany Adventure for Kids Ages 9-99 by Thomas J. Elpel. Teaches plant identification skills through an extended metaphor, an easier version of the "Botany in a Day" book below. ☻ ☻ Eyewitness: Plant by David Burnie. ☻ Wicked Plants by Amy Stewart. A fun, entertaining and easy read about poisonous plants that have made history. ☻ Botany in a Day by Thomas J. Elpel. Requires some effort, but if you're serious about learning to identify plants in the field, this is the book for you. Contains evolutionary material. ☻ The Botany Coloring Book by Paul Young. A detailed coloring book of science for older kids and adults.
The Arts	Search for: ancient Peruvian art, ancient Peru art, ancient Andes art, ancient South America art, Chavin art, Moche art, Nazca lines ☻ The Art of Ancient Peru by Shirley Glubok. ☻ Art of the Andes: from Chavin to Inca by Rebecca R. Stone.

History: Ancient South America

Teaching Tip

If you have kids of different ages, you don't have to dumb down the information for the little ones. Just let them join in as they can. When they get frustrated just help them out, like writing while they narrate instead of expecting them to write or letting them go off and play during a long video on a topic over their heads. Just relax and let learning be fun and they'll want to be there for the education. Besides, kids can understand way more than you'd think.

Additional Layer

Jaguars, snakes, and eagles were all considered sacred animals by many South American cultures. Learn more about these animals.

The oldest known civilizations of the Andes were the Norte Chico peoples in Ecuador. They began as small villages, then expanded into cities with trading, well developed religion, social classes, and big temple complexes, including pyramids.

Site of a Norte Chico City.

The Norte Chico were building their pyramids at about the same time the Egyptians built pyramids, and their cities were at their height at the time Mesopotamia was emerging into civilization. Many of their practices and beliefs are a mystery. Archaeologists have only buildings, carvings, and a few fragments of pottery, jewelry, and baskets to go off of. They did apparently practice human sacrifice and ritual cannibalism in their final centuries as a civilization. Overall, they followed the tradition of thousands of civilizations all over the world and went from simple farmers to villagers and moved into cities, after which an elite class rose up, claiming a mandate from God to control the society. They quickly descended into evil practices and shortly thereafter disappeared from the archaeological record.

Next came the Chavin in roughly the same area as the Norte Chico people. They built cities and temples and learned metallurgy, and how to carve in stone as the people before and after them had. They domesticated llamas and cultivated potatoes, maize, and quinoa using irrigation. There is evidence that, over time, they went from being a rural society to being an urban one. Archaeologists believe the elite lived in cities in the western, lower elevations and that food was brought to them from the higher elevation rural population. The religious elite consolidated power by changing the traditions and religious beliefs of the people. Some of the changes included using drugs in religious ceremonies to create hallucinations, building exclusive walled gardens and walled galleries open to only a few, and keeping the elite and the masses separate from each other. They, too, quickly fell after reaching the height of their power, wealth, and wickedness.

The Chavin people were followed by the Moche in the same area of Ecuador. They rose up, got rich, and fell in the same way as the people before them. Before they fizzled out they built cities and traded with people as far away as the Maya in central America. They had elaborate burials and made ceramic pottery using molds, which indicates mass production. They also indulged in obscene religious rituals before the end came for them.

The Canari people lived further north and even higher in the Andes, in what is now Ecuador. They were a thriving people until the Inca conquered them and made them a vassal state. Their capital city is believed to have been el Dorado, the "City of Gold" the Spanish obsessed about, but it was looted and destroyed by first the Inca, and then the Spanish themselves.

The Tiwanaku lived on the southern end of lake Titicaca in Bolivia. One of their cities has been excavated at that site. They built pyramids of stone and practiced raised field farming, where they dug ditches and raised the land between to drain off wet lands to make farm lands. They had water-filled ditches with water plants and fisheries. They traded all over the southern Andes. They disappeared long before the Incas showed up on the scene; when they found the abandoned city they fancied it was the birthplace of mankind and reverenced it as a holy site.

Next, back up north on the border between Panama and Colombia there lived the Chibchas people. They probably migrated from Central America and settled both in the lowlands near the sea and higher in the mountains. They farmed, mined salt and emeralds, and traded with other peoples. Their religion was pantheistic and involved sacrifices of wealth, food, and sometimes even human life. They existed from ancient times until the Spanish conquistadors came.

Additional Layer

For a long time scholars thought the Amazon region had always been sparsely populated like it is today, but recent finds indicate that it was actually rather densely populated. More recent estimates predict that between 5 and 7 million people lived there before the Europeans came with their diseases.

In 1542, a Spaniard named Francisco de Orellana traveled the Amazon from the Andes in Peru to the sea. He reported that there was a flourishing and large culture of natives living in the jungles. No one believed him because just a few years later they had all disappeared.

Fabulous Fact

The Canari people of Ecuador are still there. The direct descendants of these people didn't intermarry much with the Spaniards and other Europeans who came to the area.

Additional Layer

The Canari had a system of government where there was a supreme king or high kings and then there were smaller kings who ruled over particular tribes. The petty kings ruled independently until a national emergency came along, then they united under the high king. This sort of government is called a federated monarchy.

The United States was founded as a federal republic. What do you think this means, and is it still a federal republic?

Fabulous Fact

Here's a guess at how a village in ancient Cañaris might have looked.

Photo by Cayambe and shared on Wikimedia.

The stone has a notch in the top that catches light and acts as a calendar. At different times of the day it creates a shadow that can look like a puma, a condor, and a snake.

And now we move on to the Amazon Basin. Archaeologists had always believed the Amazon has been virgin jungle with just a few nomadic tribes subsisting in various places until 2003 when a large cluster of villages was found that must have supported many thousands of people. Since that find, a few other locations of sedentary peoples have been found in the Amazon, many as old and as advanced as any in the Andes Mountains. The Amazon cities were built of wood and clay (instead of stone) and were quickly swallowed by the jungle after their people died off or faded away. One fascinating aspect of these sites is that the soil in many raised and obviously human cultivated sites is far superior to the jungle soil as a whole. Archaeologists believe this terra preta, or black soil, may constitute as much as 15% of the Amazon Basin, an area larger than France. Since the finds are so new, there is very little we know about these people so far, except they had large cities, large fields, roads, bridges, and amphitheaters.

Amazonian earthworks revealed after sections of rainforest have been cleared. Photo by Sanna Saunaluoma and shared on Wikimedia.

EXPLORATION: Ancient South American Civilizations Map

Make a map showing some of the ancient sites of civilization in South America. Use the South America map from the end of this unit.

Label these civilizations:

- Cañaris
- Chibchas
- Amazon
- Norte Chico
- Chavin
- Moche
- Tiwanaku

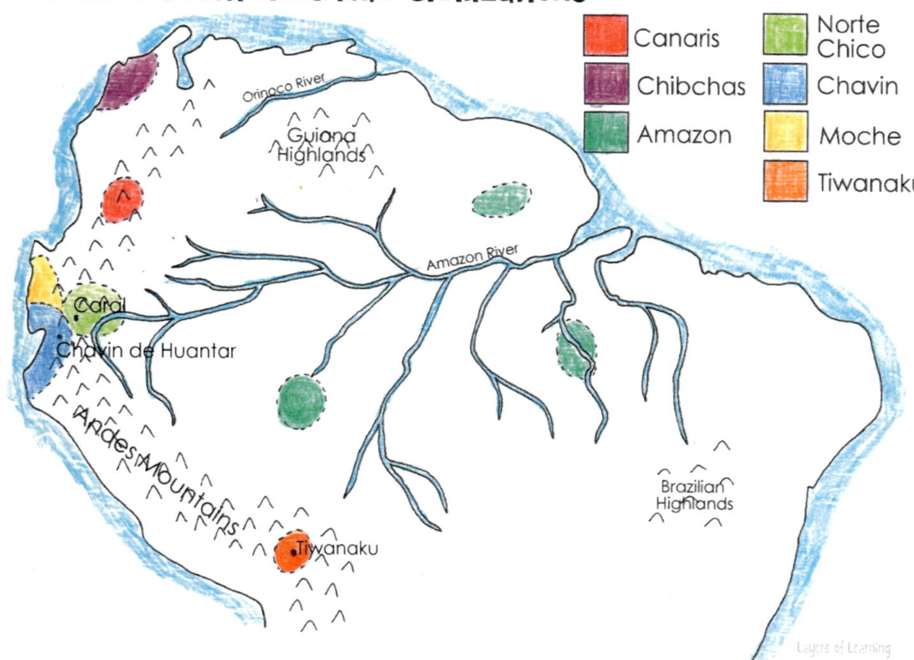

Additional Layer

Late in the history of the Canari, they were subjugated by the Incas. The Canari living within the Inca Empire allied with Pissaro and helped to bring about the defeat of the Inca.

Additional Layer

People think of the Incas as an ancient South American civilization, but they weren't. They actually started about the same time Columbus was discovering the Americas and their rule only lasted a brief hundred years.

EXPLORATION: Ancient South American Timeline

Make a timeline of ancient South America starting with these dates, which are very approximate. Many civilizations are so recently found that there are no dates as yet. You will find printable timeline squares at the end of this unit.

- 2600-2000 BC Norte Chico civilization at its height
- 900 – 200 BC Chavin civilization
- 400 BC – 1200 AD Tiwanaku civilization
- 100 – 800 AD Moche civilization

EXPLORATION: Scraps of History

The little dots on the map in this unit show just a few of the ancient civilizations. There are more we know about and many more we do not. It is likely that the entire continent was claimed by various nations just as land throughout Europe was claimed. But we've found almost no written records and by the time Europeans thought to write down what they saw, they had destroyed nearly all of it, including the people. What we do know comes from a few prominent buildings, some shards of pottery, pieces of baskets, and burial sites.

Imagine if two thousand years from now someone stumbles across the remains of your town and all they find is the cemetery

Teaching Tip

When is the last time you assessed how you're doing? At the beginning of each year, write down what you want your children to learn in order of importance. Include life skills and spiritual and character stuff as well as academics. Take a look at it every now and then to reassess how you're doing. Be deliberate in your education.

Michelle

and the ruins of city hall. What would they think of you? Write a story as though you are that future archaeologist making that find.

EXPLORATION: Jaguar's Roar

During the rainy season water would be funneled away from the temple in the Chavin capital city through specially built canals. As it rushed through it sounded like the Jaguar temple was roaring.

Jaguars and eagles were the mascots of choice for the Chavin and for other South American peoples, though none lived in their area. Make a jaguar mask from a paper plate and the template from the end of this unit. Just print the mask, color it, glue it to a paper plate, cut out holes for eyes, and attach some brightly colored feathers if you'd like.

EXPLORATION: Embroidery 101

Peoples from several of the South American areas were skilled weavers and embroiderers. The Paracas people of Peru made beautiful embroideries and used them to wrap their loved ones who had died.

Using a small piece of cloth, a needle, and various colors of embroidery floss. Make a simple design. You can even trace one of these on to the cloth and then stitch around it to help you.

Additional Layer

The powerful Harpy Eagle is native to South and Central America.

Photo by Tom Friedel at http://www.birdphotos.com/ and shared under cc license.

Additional Layer

Cassava is a plant originally from South America grown in the tropical regions there for food. It has been exported all over the world and is grown as a main staple in most of the developing world, like Africa and parts of Asia. You probably are familiar with at least one product from this plant, tapioca, often served in pudding.

Image by Amada44 and shared on Wikimedia.

What other South American plants have saved the world from hunger?

Additional Layer
Read some of the Llama Llama books by Anna Dewdney for cute stories about an adorable little llama.

Fabulous Facts
Did you know llamas make great guard animals?

South American farmers used the dung of camelids to fertilize their crops. We still use animal dung for this purpose.

Additional Layer
If you were an ancient South American kid you might get served a dinner of guinea pig meat.

Photo by RK , CC license

Mmmmm . . .

☺ ☻ **EXPLORATION: Alpaca Craft**

To make an alpaca craft, cut each edge off of a white paper plate. The cut edges become the ears. You can staple them on to the top of your little fella. Next, cut out one section of a white egg carton and glue it on in the nose spot. Finally, decorate him with cotton balls for fur and buttons for his eyes and nose.

Write a story about yourself as an alpaca farmer to go along with your alpaca craft. Imagine that you must go on a long journey and your Alpaca will be your only traveling companion. Outline the beginning, middle, and end of your storyline first, then write your story.

Expedition

Alpacas were first exported out of South America in the 1980's. Since then their fibers have become very popular all over the world. It is soft, water proof, and warm. It isn't scratchy or full of lanolin like sheep's wool. And alpacas are friendly, gentle animals. Find out if there is an alpaca farm near you and see if you can arrange for a visit.

Additional Layer

How can animals be "cousins"? What people mean is that animals have similar features, typological (the way they look) and/or a similar genetic code.

Evolutionists mean that these animal "cousins" descended from the same ultimate ancestor back in the dark past of evolution.

So how did camel and alpacas on two completely separate and isolated continents come to be related?

Some theorize that the animals developed on the American continent and spread via the land bridge in the Bering Strait. What do you think?

EXPLORATION: South American Crops

Many of the foods we still enjoy today were grown by ancient South Americans in the Amazon Basin. Go to the grocery store and get squash, chiles, and beans to sample. All of those were crops grown thousands of years ago, and we still grow them today. If you're really adventurous you might even try getting some seeds for these crops and growing your own South American vegetable.

EXPLORATION: Camelids

Llamas, vicunas, guanacos, and alpacas were all camelids (cousins of the camel) that were domesticated by these ancient peoples. They are some of the oldest domesticated animals in the world. They were used to transport goods, and also kept for their wool and meat.

Choose one of these species to research more about. They are all related, but each species has some unique characteristics too. Once you've gathered some information, make a Powerpoint presentation or slide show showing what you know.

EXPLORATION: Canals

The people of Norte Chico lived in an unlikely area – very dry with little access to important natural resources. They couldn't have existed at all without a system of irrigation canals that brought them water.

Use a sand box. Start with a lot of water in one corner and challenge the kids to get water across the sandbox to a marked location. For older kids, put numbered flags in different areas of the sandbox, then have the kids try to route water through canals they build from one flag to the next, in order.

☻ ☻ ☻ EXPLORATION: Nazca Lines

The Nazca people (also known as Nasca) made giant outlines of animals and other shapes in the deserts of Peru. The lines were scratched into the surface of the dirt. They are so large that it is actually difficult to see them when you're nearby, but an aerial view shows a clear picture. They were actually discovered when commercial flights began to operate in a path over where the lines were.

Go visit the Nazca article on National Geographic's website. It's an excellent look into the Nazca people, the mysterious patterns they left on the ground, and what their civilization may have been like, along with neat photos and animations. You'll find it at: http://ngm.nationalgeographic.com/2010/03/nasca/hall-text/1

Once you've read the article and explored the information there, create your own Nazca line art. Design a simple motif that could be carved into the ground, then write about its significance. There is another Nazca lines exploration in the arts section of this unit.

Additional Layer

Ancient South Americans built aqueducts to transport water. Here is the entrance to one aqueduct in the Nazca Desert of Peru.

Learn more about aqueducts and how they work to transport water. Which civilizations built them and are they still used today?

Additional Layer

This is a representation of an eagle that was found on the cornice of a building from the Chavin culture. It was a stone carving. Creation of art in a civilization means that the people were settled, fed, and safe enough to have leisure time and be able to focus on beauty and not just survival. You'll find this coloring sheet in the printables section.

Geography: South America

Memorization Station

Memorize the countries and capitals of South America and their location. Use puzzles, maps, online quiz games, and songs.

Fabulous Fact

One third of the continent of South America is covered by the Amazon Rain Forest.

Additional Layer

In 2005, leaders from all but two of South America's nations met to enter into a European style economic and military alliance called the Union of South American Nations. Their goal is to have duty free trade, a common currency, common passports, open borders, and a military alliance.

All but French Guiana and Panama have joined the union.

South America lies across the equator. The north is wet, dense jungle; the south is grasslands that taper into an alpine climate. The Andes Mountains which run the entire length of the continent from north to south are also alpine. The Pacific coastal region is mostly desert.

There are 13 countries in South America. Most are Spanish-speaking since the Spanish ruled much of continent for several hundred years. Brazil is Portuguese-speaking and in French Guiana, French is spoken. Many South American countries, having centralized economies, are struggling with poverty. A few, like Chile, are doing better. Economic problems and corruption in government have meant big drug problems with powerful criminal drug cartels exporting their products, mostly to North America. The people of South America are descended partly from natives and partly from Spanish and Portuguese settlers. There are still aboriginal tribes living in some parts of the Amazon River Basin and Patagonia.

☺ ☻ **EXPLORATION: Fabric Map**

Make a physical map out of fabric scraps. First, draw, trace, or print out an outline of the continent. Cut out small bits of dark green, light green, brown, yellow, and blue fabric. Glue the fabric onto the paper outline. Draw the rivers on with blue fabric paint.

Brown = mountains
Dark Green = jungle
Light Green = grassland or farmland
Yellow = desert
Blue = lakes and oceans

☺ ☻ **EXPLORATION: Animal Collage**

Make a collage of South American animals. Print a bunch from the Internet or cut them out of nature magazines.

EXPLORATION: South American Map

Color a physical map of South America. Print the South America Physical Map from the end of this unit. Use a student atlas and label the major bodies of water, mountains, and physical features.

Freshwater:
- Amazon River
- Paraguay River
- Lake Titicaca

Seas:
- Pacific Ocean
- Atlantic Ocean
- Antarctic Ocean

Land Features:
- Andes Mountains
- Guiana Highlands
- Patagonia
- Pampas
- Amazon Basin

EXPLORATION: Political Map

Color a political map of South America, which you will find at the end of this unit. Label the countries and capitals of South America. Find images of South America from magazines or online and place them around the map.

Countries:
- Colombia
- Ecuador
- A Peru
- Bolivia
- Chili
- Argentina
- Uruguay
- Paraguay
- JD Brazil
- Venezuela
- M Guyana
- Suriname
- French Guiana

Cities:
- Bogota
- Quito
- Lima
- La Paz
- Santiago
- Buenos Aires
- Montevideo
- Sao Paulo
- Brasilia
- Caracas
- Georgetown

EXPLORATION: Geo Gamer

Visit www.kids.nationalgeographic.com for geography games that cover the whole world.

EXPLORATION: GOAL!

Soccer is big, big, big in South America, only they call it fútbol. Learn how to play and have a backyard game with your family or friends.

Additional Layer

Lake Titicaca in Bolivia is covered with man-made floating islands upon which the people live and grow gardens.

The first floating islands were built by pre-Incan people who wanted to get out of paying taxes!

Additional Layer

South American governments are all modern democracies in name, but the reality has been upheaval, military coups, drug lords, lawlessness, and rampant corruption.

Why does stable government elude some countries and places in the world? Think about that as you learn about countries.

President Lula of Brazil, President Kirchner of Argentina and President Chavez of Venezuela.

Teaching Tip

Learning how to do research in a library is one of the most important skills students can learn. We can never teach them all there is to know about every subject, but if we teach them how to learn and find things out on their own, we're giving them a priceless gift.

Famous Folks

Ernesto "Che" Guevara was an Argentinian medical student who traveled Latin America witnessing poverty and suffering. He got mad about it and decided the best option was global revolution and the ushering in of communism, including Castro in Cuba.

Some people see Che as a rebel hero of the masses and others revile him as a destroyer of human life and happiness. Learn more. What do you think?

☻ ☻ ☻ EXPLORATION: South American Cuisine

Some favorite foods that came from South America include potatoes, cocoa (chocolate), coffee beans, sweet potatoes, lima beans, hot peppers and many, many types of fruit. Nearly everybody in South America eats some kind of flat bread. Either thin tortillas or thicker arepas.

You can make your own tortillas at home.

You'll need:

- 5 cups flour
- 1 Tbsp. Salt
- ½ cup shortening
- 2 cups water

1. Mix the four ingredients together thoroughly using a stand mixer or pastry tool. Divide the dough into 24 chunks. Cover them with a kitchen towel so they don't dry out.
2. One at a time, roll out each piece of dough into a thin, round shape (mine are never perfectly round – it's okay!). Place the round of dough on to a hot, ungreased griddle. Cook each one until it bubbles up and just barely gets a brown spot or two. Flip over and cook for about a minute on the other side.
3. Continue rolling out and cooking each tortilla one by one. Store them in a sealed plastic bag in the fridge.

EXPLORATION: Angel Falls

Angel Falls is the highest waterfall in the world. You'd have to hike through the Venezuelan rain forest to see it.

Go pay a visit to You Tube and see the majesty of Angel Falls. BBC made a beautiful clip showing the majesty of the falls at http://youtu.be/BVR5CvekD7s
You can also see some brave people base jumping down near the falls at http://youtu.be/hT0UewyAz0o
Seeing this in person is on my bucket list.

EXPLORATION: Continent Researcher

Use the Continent Research Form from the printables at http://www.layers-of-learning.com/continent-research-worksheet/ to help you organize a research project about South America. Head to the library with your sheet and get some information the good old fashioned way – from books.

EXPLORATION: Country Lapbook

Choose one of the South American countries and make a lapbook about it. Start with a file folder. Color a map, create a flag, and use the country fact sheet on the printables page of www.Layers-of-Learning.com. Just fill in each of the boxes on the printable, cut them out, and paste them to the file folder. Decorate and fill

Fabulous Facts

The Nile River may be the longest in the world, but the Amazon carries more than twice as much water.

South America is the fourth largest continent.

Approximately 3.7 million people live in South America today.

The only country in South America that is not independent is French Guiana, which is a department of France.

Ushuaia, Argentina is the southernmost city in the world.

Venezuela is Spanish for "little Venice." The native people there built stilt houses on water reminding Europeans of Venice, also built on water.

Additional Layer

The Andes Range is part of the Pacific Ring of Fire, a giant circle of volcanoes surrounding much of the Pacific Ocean.

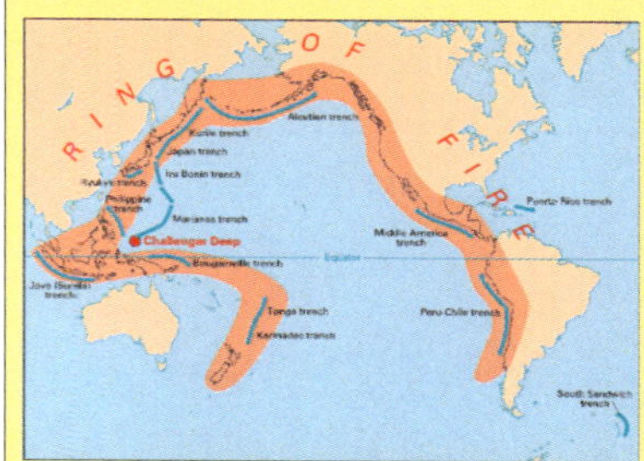

Do you think there are volcanoes and earthquakes there?

in all the blanks on your file folder with other details and fun facts about the country. If you'd like to, you can create little pockets and flip-ups to house some of your details. Make it colorful and fun!

EXPLORATION: Carnival

Carnival is a traditional celebration that comes just before Lent. It usually involves a parade and lots of partying. Rio de Janeiro, Brazil hosts the biggest carnival celebration in the whole world. People wear ornate costumes and dance and parade down the streets of the city. Tourists come from around the world, not just to see it, but to participate in the party. Many spend hundreds of dollars to buy appropriate costumes so they'll be able to join in with the parade groups.

Make a poster advertising Carnival and highlighting all the festivities.

EXPLORATION: Lake Titicaca

Lake Titicaca is the largest lake in South America and is also the highest navigable lake in the world. There are actually dozens of lakes that are higher, but they are all much smaller. Lake Titicaca is large enough for commercial ships to navigate. It is up so high because it is situated in the Andes Mountains on the border of Bolivia and Peru. The people who live there have built floating islands out of the reeds that grow there naturally.

There are several excellent documentaries about Lake Titicaca on

Famous Folks

Born Edson Arantes do Nascimento, Pelé of Brazil is arguably the best fútbol player to ever have lived.

Writer's Workshop

Pretend you have just gone to Carnival. Write a journal entry about all you saw and did.

Additional Layer

A lot of people are worried about deforestation in the rainforests. Learn more about this. Is it a problem? What are the consequences of deforestation? Who gets hurt if no new farmland can be cleared? What solutions can you see to the problem?

Additional Layer

Bolivia is a landlocked country, but it has a navy! They do drills and naval exercises on Lake Titicaca.

You Tube. For a quick tour check out these videos:

- http://youtu.be/2729LQajLiE
- http://youtu.be/kAEzKGwYELc

EXPEDITION: Andes Mountains

The Andes Mountain Range is long! In fact, it's the longest of all the continental mountain ranges. Take a look at a globe or map and figure out about how many miles it runs. It goes right up the western coastline of South America.

Since ancient times people have lived high in the Andes mountains. To do this, they had to terrace the mountainsides to create many, small flat areas to farm.

One of the main crops grown was the potato. It is indigenous to South America. They actually grow over 200 varieties of potato there (including blue ones!).

Go to a local grocery store in your town and see how many varieties of potato you can find. Choose some to buy and bring home to bake and play with. Wash each potato, wrap it in foil, and bake it for about an hour at 350 degrees. You can put lots of toppings on your potato. Choose from: ground beef, sour cream, dressings, cheeses, chili, butter, seasonings and spices, chives, or other favorites. While you're eating, think of as many other ways to cook potatoes as you can – mashed potatoes, french fries, potato soup . . . the list goes on and on.

You can also use potatoes for stamping. Start by cutting the potato in half. Stick a cookie cutter into the open face of the potato. Carefully cut away the potato around the cookie cutter to create your stamping surface.

Additional Layer

Ponchos are a traditional piece of South American clothing. They are a small rectangular blanket with a hole in the center for the head. They drape over the body and can be pulled tight for warmth. If made of water repellent materials they can also keep the wearer dry.

Here is a photo of the Brazilian president in a poncho.

Photo taken by Marcello Cassal Jr. of the Agência Brasil, a Brazilian News Agency.

Potatoes might never have caught on in Europe if it weren't for Marie Antoinette who wore a garland of potato blossoms on her hat and Frederick the Great who planted them in his personal garden and touted their healthful properties.

Fabulous Fact

About 200 different Amazonian fruits are cultivated for human use, but there are more than 3,000 varieties of edible fruits growing there in the wild.

A fruit called "Bacuri."

Additional Layer

In this world of satellite pictures of the whole earth, of airplanes, of the Internet, of modern vehicles and roads and über-big government bureaucracies, it is absolutely astounding that in 2011 a tribe of 200 people living in the Amazon on the Brazil-Peru border were discovered.

Anthropologists estimate that at least 14 more tribes never before contacted may be living in this area as well.

Brazil's policy is one of isolation. It is illegal to contact the tribesmen in any way, as the government fears introducing disease.

What do you think?

Then dip the potato lightly into paint and stamp it on a big sheet of paper. You can use the stamp over and over to repeat your design.

EXPLORATION: Amazon River

The Amazon River is the second longest river in the world. It is home to many interesting species of fish and animals, and also the home to indigenous tribes. There are tribes of natives there who have no contact with the outside world, living very simply.

Do some Internet research on the Amazon Basin area. Find out what it's like and then do an oral report about what you learned.

EXPLORATION: Amazon Rainforest

The Amazon Rainforest is home to over one third of all the animal species in the world. Rainforests are one of our most important resources because of the biodiversity within them.

Use the rainforest coloring sheet at the back of this unit and draw in your own animals showing some that live in the Amazon Rainforest. If you don't know how to draw them, just do an Internet search for "how to draw ____________"(fill in the animal name) and you'll likely find a tutorial.

Science: Plants

Plants are classified and put into groups just like animals, geographical formations, types of elements, or anything else that people come across. We really like order. At the top of the classification system are the "kingdoms," and plants are one of the five kingdoms. The next level down is the division, then the class, order, family, genus, and species. Sometimes sub-classes, sub-kingdoms, and so on are also added to give more description. When scientists speak about a particular plant they use the genus and species name.

Plants are in their own kingdom because they can take energy from the sun and they have rigid cell walls, where animals have soft cells.

Four Divisions of Plants

Plants are first put into divisions, the number and arrangement of which is debatable. There are four main divisions you should know about: mosses, ferns, conifers, and flowering plants. Next, the flowering plants are divided into monocotyledon and dicotyledons. Dicots have two leaves that emerge from the seed and monocots have just one leaf that emerges from the seed. Finally, plants are further defined by the number of petals on their flowers, the shape of their leaves, their growing patterns and other things.

Explanation

A roller box is a box with 2 dowels that hold a scroll of paper. Pictures, words, clues, or ANYTHING can be added to the scroll. Then when it's rolled along the kids get to see what's "playing on the box" that day.

Use it to introduce a new topic, review a topic you're finishing off, show your timeline, make a report more fun, or display some cool stuff you've done lately.

You could also add pictures and facts to it as you go throughout a unit, then "watch" it as a review at the end.

Memorization Station

There is some controversy about where to place plants in the classification scheme, but we'll give you four main plant divisions to memorize:

Bryophyte – mosses: non-vascular, spores, no flowers

Pteridophyta – ferns: vascular, spores, no flowers

Coniferophyta – conifers: cones & needles, seeds, no flowers, vascular

Magnoliophyta – flowering plants: seeds, vascular, flowers

Additional Layer

Selective weed killing chemicals that you may spread on your lawn in the spring work because they attack only plants that are dicotyledons. Monocots (your grass) aren't harmed but dandelions, clover, and other weeds get it. Research more about the way weed killers work and what effect they have on the environment other than the weeds they are targeted to kill. You may be surprised.

Here is the classification for a dandelion:

Kingdom	Plantae	Plants
Division	Magnoliophyta	Flowering plants
Class	Magnoliopsida	Dicots
Order	Asterales	
Family	Asteraceae	Aster family
Genus	Taraxacum	Dandelion
Species	Officinale	Common

So if you as a botanist (plant scientist) were to write a paper on the dandelion you would call it *Taraxacum officinale* and sound very intelligent.

☻ ☻ EXPERIMENT: Tasty Model Plant Cell

Make a model of a plant cell. You need a package of green jello, some peas, peanuts, a grape, and a small box. Prepare the jello and pour into a zipper top sandwich bag until about half full. Add one grape, ten peas, and six peanuts. Place it into the jello box with one side cut off. Place in the fridge to firm up.

The box is the rigid sides of the cell, made of cellulose. The plastic bag represents the plasma membrane. The grape is the nucleus, or central command of the cell. The peanuts are the mitochondria, or energy production of the cell. The peas are the chloroplasts, or sunlight capturing parts of the cell. And the jello is the cytoplasm, the stuff the cell parts float around in.

☻ ☻ EXPERIMENT: Under a Microscope

Look at actual plant cells. You need a microscope for this one.

1. Cut a very thin slice of onion, one layer thick.
2. Place it in a drop of water on a microscope slide, under a slide cover.
3. Look at it through the microscope.
4. You can see square boxes and possibly dots in the middle of the boxes.

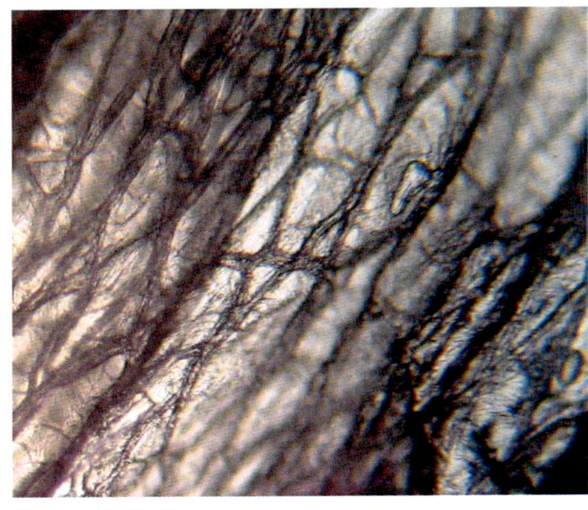

The boxes are called cells and the dots in the middle are the nuclei. The monk who first discovered plant cells called them cells because they look like little

rooms, or cells in a monastery all lined up.
Scientific supply stores like *Home Science Tools* sell microscopes and prepared slides for home use.

EXPERIMENT: Permeable Plasma
The plasma membrane is permeable. That means stuff can pass through it – like gases, water, and nutrients. To demonstrate this, get a zipper closed sandwich bag. Place a few drops of scented liquid (like mint extract or vanilla extract) into the bag. Seal it and place it in a plastic container with a lid. Let it sit for 20 minutes then lift the lid of the container and sniff. You should smell the mint or vanilla. The plastic bag seals out some things, but lets other things through. It is permeable.

EXPERIMENT: Permeability of a Raisin
Another example of permeability can be seen with raisins. Place several raisins in a cup of water for a day. They will fill with water right through the skin. The skin is permeable to water.

EXPLORATION: Photosynthesis
Make a diagram showing how photosynthesis gives plants energy.

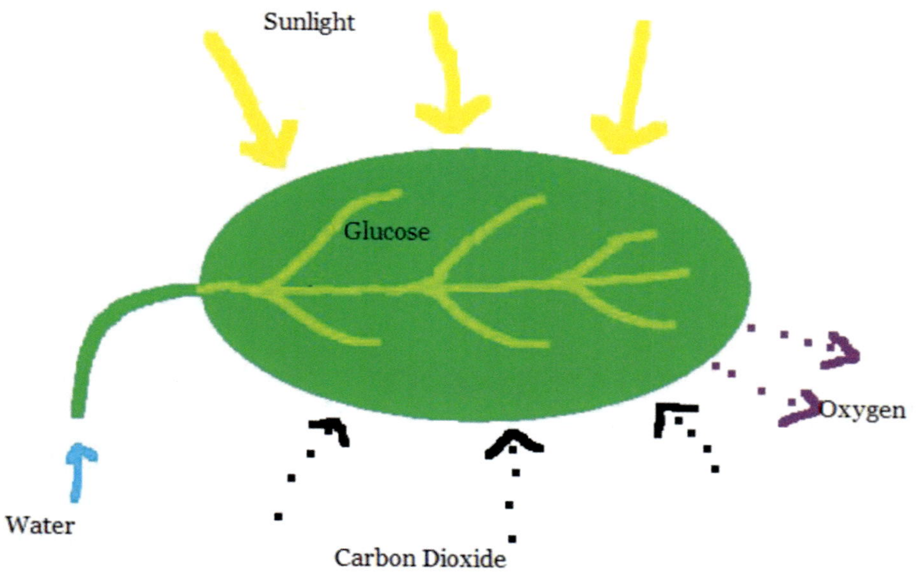

Plants breath carbon dioxide in through special pores on the underside of their leaves called stomata. They pull water up from the ground through their roots and vascular system and both carbon dioxide and water are brought to the cells of the leaves. They pass through the membrane and into the cytoplasm where they are met with energy from the sun that has been collected by chlorophyll. The chlorophyll converts light energy into chemical

Additional Layer

Onions make you cry because when you cut the cells walls you release chemicals that were previously kept separate in the onion, producing a volatile sulfur vapor. When it gets in your eyes it makes sulfuric acid.

On The Web

Are you new to gardening? Perhaps you just want to be more organized and maybe try some new things. We discovered a site called Sprout Robot. You can sign up for free and they'll send you e-mail reminders about what to plant in your zone and when. They also tell you when it's the right time for fertilizing, trimming, harvesting, and tilling.

http://sproutrobot.com/

Printable

For a printable scientific method worksheet you can fill out as you complete these experiments, head over to Layers of Learning:

http://www.layers-of-learning.com/a-simple-introduction-to-the-scientific-method/

energy and causes a reaction to occur between the water and carbon dioxide.

Here is the chemical process that takes place:

$$6CO_2 + 6H_2O \rightarrow C_6H_{12}O_6 + 6O_2$$

carbon dioxide + water → glucose + oxygen

EXPERIMENT: Terrarium

Make a self contained terrarium. Place soil, a few plants, and water into a large jar or clear container and cover with a lid or plastic. Make sure it gets sunlight, but don't open the top for several weeks. The closed system will have enough water and the plant can make its own food as long as it has sunlight. The plant would eventually die when it ran out of nutrients in the soil. If you fertilize it every six weeks or so, it can live for a very long time without having to be watered.

Make a poster showing the things a plant needs to survive.

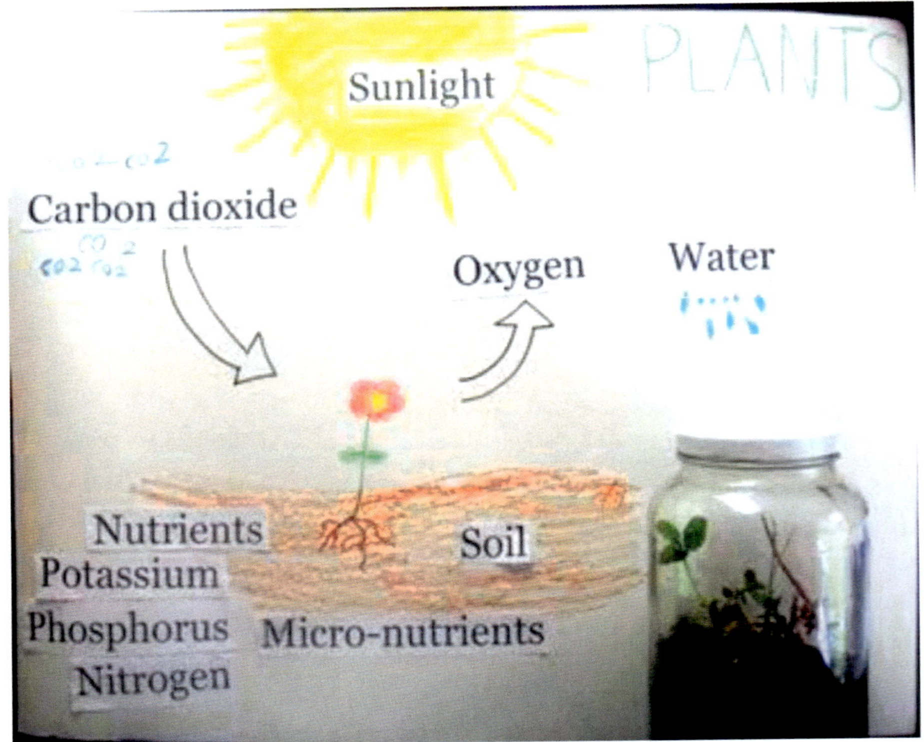

EXPERIMENT: Just Breathe

Prove that plants breathe through their leaves. Use a house plant and thickly coat the tops of four leaves with Vaseline. Coat the bottoms of three leaves with Vaseline. Make predictions about

Famous Folks

Carl Linnaeus, a Swedish scientist, invented the classification system using Latin and the descending levels of grouping organisms plus the binomial system of using two names for each organism.

Portrait by Johan Henrik Scheffel, 1739

On The Web

Extend your plant lesson into art by making a crayon batik of a plant terrarium covered with watercolor paints.

Visit http://www.artprojectsforkids.org/2008/05/plants-in-jar.html for complete directions.

what you expect to have happen. Observe the leaves over several days. What happens to them? The holes on leaves that plants breathe through are tiny, like the pores on your skin. We call them stomata.

EXPERIMENT: Don't Spill the Beans

Soak some bean seeds in water overnight. Open up a bean seed, splitting it in half along the seam. You will see two sides. Because the bean splits into two sides we know it is a dicotyledon. The small dark spot on the outside of the bean is called the micropyle, where the pollen entered to fertilize the seed. The larger spot on the outside of the bean is the hilum, where it was attached to the seed pod. The outer covering which protects the seed is called the seed coat. Inside the seed you see a tiny structure looking like the beginnings of a plant. This is the epicotyl (forms the first leaves, hypocaust (forms the stem) and radical (forms the roots).

After inspecting your bean seed glue it to a piece of paper and label the parts.

EXPERIMENT: Sprouting

See how a seed sprouts. Get a paper towel wet and place inside a zipper sealed plastic bag with a bean seed. The bean will sprout and the roots will grow out one end and the leaves begin to grow out the other. The bean will die once the nutrients in the seed are used up unless you plant it.

Additional Layer

Make your garden more fun and colorful by adding cute signs to all your rows.

Corny Plant Jokes

What do you call a stolen yam?

Hot Potato

What does everyone have on their faces?

Tulips

Why does a potato make a great detective?

He keeps his eyes peeled

How do you mend a pumpkin?

With a pumpkin patch

Teaching Tip

If your seeds are small enough you can plant them in a clear CD case filled with soil. This allows you to watch the roots as the seed sprouts.

Additional Layer

Soil is essential to plant growth. Learn more about soil horizons and what it takes to make plants happy.

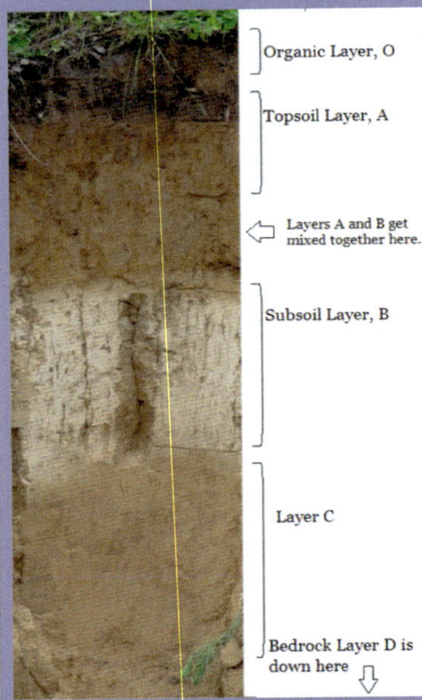

Which plants do well in soils that others can't handle?

Additional Layer

Plants are often a featured aspect of a coat of arms like this one from Germany showing onions.

What plant would you choose to represent you?

Alternatively, you could plant bean seeds in a clear plastic cup filled with soil. Place several bean seeds right against the edge of the cup so you can watch them grow. Orient some of the seeds upside right and others upside down. What happens to the roots and the leaves in each case?

EXPERIMENT: Plants All Around

Get a potted plant (or several of the same type) and place it in different environments to see how it does. What if it is kept in a dark cupboard? What if you keep it in the fridge? What if you drown the roots? What if it doesn't get watered at all?

EXPLORATION: Classification

Cut out pictures of a dozen different types of plants, or go outside and collect some. Now organize them into groups based on whatever criteria you like. You might put all plants with red flowers in a group, or you might decide that all plants with simple leaves should be together. Explain why you grouped the plants the way you did.

EXPLORATION: Plant Creator

Create a brand new plant species. Draw a picture of it, give a close up view of the leaves and the flower or cone. Based on the characteristics you give it, which division and class would your plant belong to? What genus and species name would you give it?

EXPERIMENT: Thirsty

Observe how plants draw water through their stems. You need several white carnations, glasses or jars, water, and food coloring.

Fill each glass at least half full with water and add several drops of food coloring to the water. Place a flower in the water and leave overnight. The petals will turn the color of the water.

You can do a similar experiment using celery and watch as a limp celery stalk is lifted up; you'll also be able to see holes where water was funneled up the stem of the celery.

Water moves through all plants this way, through channels in the body of the plant, picked up in the soil by the roots and drawn up to the leaves. Nutrients that plants need are dissolved in water while in the soil and brought up with the water.

Additional Layer
Christianity, ancient pantheistic religions, Buddhism, and Judaism all feature a Tree of Life.

This depiction of the Tree of Life is stained glass by Louis Comfort Tiffany.

EXPERIMENT: Too Much Water
Over watering kills plants. The stems burst from the pressure of the water that is drawn up. Pressure inside a plant is called turgor pressure. Get a stalk of rhubarb, cut a section and float it in a bowl of water overnight. In the morning the ends of the stalk will be broken and curled up. The stems have burst apart.

EXPERIMENT: Plant Press
Build a plant press and collect plants from your area over the next several weeks as you study botany.

Pressing plants is useful for making collections. You can keep the plant leaves, dried out and flattened, in a notebook or file. Here's how to make your own plant press.

1. Cut two pieces of wood so they each measure 5" by 7 ½"
2. Cut many sheets of newspaper to measure the same.
3. Cut three pieces of cardboard to measure the same as well.

Arrange the layers with wood on bottom, then paper, then cardboard, then paper, then cardboard, then paper, and finally your second piece of wood.

Additional Layer
Turn this bowl of vegetables upside down to see a portrait of the green grocer.

Painting by Giuseppe Arcimboldo.

Famous Folks

John Bartram was a largely self-educated farmer from colonial Pennsylvania turned naturalist and botanist.

Carl Linnaeus called him the "greatest natural botanist in the world."

Fabulous Fact

The largest flower in the world is the giant Rafflesia from Southeast Asia. It can weigh up to 25 pounds, is parasitic and smells like rotten meat.

Assemble the plant press with one piece of wood on the bottom, then cardboard, then a stack of newspaper, more cardboard, more newspaper, more cardboard and more newspaper, then finally your second piece of wood goes on top. Once all the pieces are assembled, place two heavy duty rubber bands around the press, one at each end. Your child can decorate the "cover" with paint if you wish.

When you place plants in, put them between sheets of newspaper. Don't place more than one layer of plants in each section of newspaper. To dry your leaves, leave them in a warm, dry place for at least three days. Check them to be sure they are dry, and if not, leave them for a couple more days.

Glue your leaves to paper, label them with the type of plant and the date and location of collection. Then place them in a book or a file.

EXPLORATION: Mary, Mary, Quite Contrary
Grow a garden. Plant vegetables or flowers. Focus on these lessons throughout the growing season:

- Plant care: fertilizer, water, sunlight, good soil
- Plant science: photosynthesis, transport, how deep to plant seeds based on the size of the seed
- Farming and food production as an industry
- Insects: observing, collect, and discover the pros and cons of various visitors to your garden
- Companion planting: how certain plants help each other when planted nearby (For example, marigolds planted by tomatoes keep many of the pest insects from eating your tomatoes because the smell of marigolds repels them.)
- Responsibility and general principles of hard work, and hopefully recognition of some of the rewards of work
- Cooking using fresh ingredients from the garden

EXPLORATION: Plant Observer
Get out a microscope, magnifying glass, and several plants, seeds, and sprouts to observe. Take some time just looking closely at them. Set out several books about plants as well. Peruse the books, observe the specimens, and write down all of your observations. Also write down things that you wonder and want to research more about.

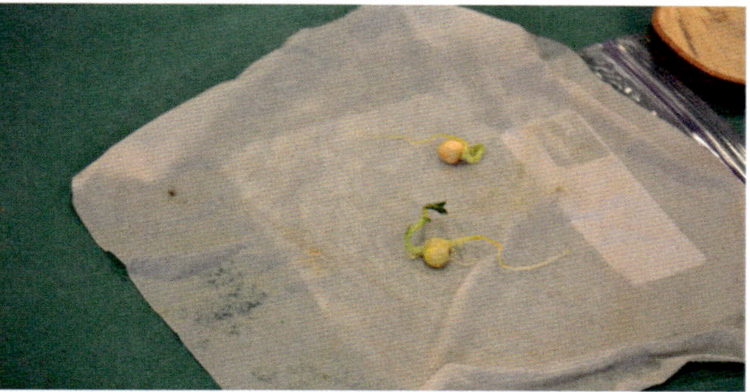

Fabulous Fact

You've heard of the Venus Fly Trap, but it's not the only carnivorous plant in the world. *Nepenthes albomarginata* traps termites and digests them in its tube shaped petals.

Light Up A Plant At Night

Normally a morning glory opens by 6:00 A.M. Keep one in the dark until 7:00 A.M., and make its day longer by shining a light on it from dusk until midnight. Place the light about 3 feet from the plant, and let it shine from dusk until midnight for about a week. At midnight, turn the light off and make sure the room is totally dark. At 7:00 A.M. let sunlight into the room. Watch what happens.

The Arts: South American Art

On The Web
The largest collection of ancient South American art is at the Museo Larco in Lima, Peru. View much of the art online: http://www.museolarco.org/visita-el-museo/historia-del-museo-larco/

Additional Layer

Like the ancient South Americans, ancient Egyptians also often incorporated half-man, half-animals figures in their art.

Additional Layer

This is ancient Peruvian fabric made from camelid hair.

Like the history of ancient South Americans, we don't know a whole lot about their art either. We have found several artifacts and make educated guesses about what we see, but because we don't have written records, we don't have much to go off of. We know about these peoples, but much of what their lives were like is still a mystery to us. Just the same, we'll do several explorations and take a look at a few things we do know.

☻ ☻ ☻ **EXPLORATION: Pottery**
Pottery is one of the most plentiful of the South American artifacts we've found. They likely used their pottery for useful purposes as well as just artistic items. Much of the pottery is just dish-shaped, but we've also found human shaped pottery as well. They are like small figurines. Often they include animal characteristics as well.

Using clay, sculpt a small person figurine. Add at least one animal characteristic, like reptile eyes, cat fangs, or wings. What characteristics might these features represent?

EXPLORATION: Burial Cloths

Some of the ancient Peruvian peoples were known for their elaborate textiles. They created long pieces of beautiful cloth which they used to bury their dead in. Some of them measured as long as 90 feet!

Get an inexpensive flat bed sheet. Using fabric markers or crayons, cover the sheet with pictures and designs that represent who you are. You might draw scenes from your life, patterns that represent your personality traits, or even words that describe you. At the end you should have a kind of autobiographical fabric of your life.

If you use crayon, cover the crayon with a piece of flat thick paper, like from a paper grocery bag and then iron over the crayon. The wax will melt off and stick to the paper, but the color will remain behind, permanently etched onto the cloth.

The ancient peoples would then wrap the mummies of their dead in these special burial cloths. Kind of a neat way to honor and remember what their lives meant.

EXPLORATION: Polychrome Pottery

Polychrome just means many colors. Really early pottery tended to just have one color. Soon, designs were painted to make the pottery beautiful, and then as time went on, cultures usually began to use more elaborate designs and colors. The ancient peoples of the Andes mountains made beautiful polychrome ceramics.

Make your own polychrome pottery by beginning with an oven-safe plain white ceramic bowl, mug, or plate. Use colorful Sharpie markers to decorate your dish. When your design is finished, bake the dish at 350 degrees for about 20 minutes. Sharpies are non-toxic, so it's safe to eat off of.

EXPLORATION: Portrait Vases

Another form of ancient South American pottery was the portrait vase. They were used to spread ideas and beliefs. Religious scenes painted on the outsides of the vases were common, though our lack of understanding of their religions makes it difficult for us to interpret what they mean.

Fabulous Fact

The Moche people made vessels for holding liquids like this one:

Some of them are birds or jaguars or other animals and some are people. The handles and spouts are always the same, no matter the subject.

Writer's Workshop

In your writer's notebook write the story you drew on your portrait vase. Remember to use descriptive language.

On the Web

This four minute video talks about the art and architecture of the Moche people who lived in northwest South America:

http://youtu.be/vbQop-LULEg

Additional Layer

The ancient people of South America called gold the "sweat of the sun," the sun being the most holy of divinities. So gold wasn't just pretty and valuable, it was also sacred.

Crown from the Chavin culture featuring the sun god.

Fabulous Fact

In many cultures the sun god was considered the highest god, probably because our sun is the brightest thing in our sky.

Additional Layer

Most of the art, pottery, and weapons found from ancient cultures are from graves. These are also targets of grave robbers, who are after the wealth. Of course archeologists "raid" the graves as well. Is one method or motivation more valid than another? Why?

Draw a simple vase on a sheet of paper. Next, choose a story or scene from your religious beliefs to draw on your vase. Tell someone the story of your picture and what it means to you.

While you work, discuss reasons why people want to spread their religious beliefs, and how we go about doing so. Art has often been the medium for telling stories, especially religious stories. Do you have any art in your home that is religious?

☻ ☻ ☻ EXPLORATION: Gate of the Sun

The Gate of the Sun is one of the biggest artifacts of early South America. It stands almost 10 feet tall and is 13 feet wide and weighs about 10 tons! It was carved from a single giant stone. It is near Lake Titicaca near modern-day La Paz, Bolivia and depicts a large image of a god flanked by other religious symbols. Archaeologists are pretty certain that it was used as some kind of a calendar.

The god in the middle of the arch is thought by many to represent a sun god, because it has rays coming out of its face. Also, all of the other figures on the arch are looking at this central god.

Detail from the center of the gate of the Sun.

Using clay or play dough, make a mold in the shape of the sun gate. Use wooden blocks pressed into the clay to make the basic shape. Then use toothpicks or other carving material to make designs in the clay. Make geometric patterns on the sides and in the center make a sun god design. Add lots of intricate details like the ones you find on the Gate of the Sun.

Prepare plaster of Paris according to the package directions and pour into your mold. Let it set up and harden completely, then remove the clay mold.

Paint the model Gate of the Sun. You can use gray colors like the stone or you can paint it in bright colors. You never know, maybe it once was painted brightly.

EXPLORATION: Rain Sticks
Rain sticks were traditionally made by native South Americans and were believed to bring rainstorms when played.

The simple musical instruments are made from hollow sticks with nails protruding into the hollow center. When beans or other small objects are placed inside, they strike the nails and make the sound you get from tilting or shaking it. It sounds like pouring water, hence a "rain stick." Long ago, they were made from dried cactus parts that had the cactus spines removed, then driven into the cactus like nails. Pebbles were placed inside to create the sound.

You can make your own simple rain stick using a paper towel roll tube. Along the diagonal seam, draw a dot about every ½ inch. Drive 1 inch nails through each dot. Cut out 2 paper circles large enough to cover the ends of the paper towel roll and secure one with tape. Duct tape, masking tape, or packaging tape work well. Place tiny pebbles or dried beans inside. Secure the other end with the second paper circle and more tape.

Additional Layer

Feathers have had spiritual significance among northern Native American tribes, the people of India, and others.

Scottish clan chiefs can earn the right to wear eagle feathers as part of their uniform.

Additional Layer

The spines injected into a rain stick are arranged helically, or like an upward moving spiral. You can show how a helix is arranged with a toilet paper roll and some string.

Look around your house and see if you can find any helically arranged objects . . . a spring, tendrils on a climbing vine, a spiral staircase, or a spiral twist on an iron railing.

Writer's Workshop

No one knows why the Nasca lines were made or who made them. Wild theories include an ancient advanced civilization capable of flight, aliens in UFO's, ancient race tracks, and giants. Come up with a wild theory of your own and write it down in your Writer's Notebook.

Additional Layer

The giant of Atacama, a geoglyph etched onto the side of a desert mountain in Chili's Atacama desert is 393 feet tall.

Photograph by Emilio and shared on Wikimedia.

Additional Layer

Not all of the Nasca lines are shaped like animals or people, many of them are just long straight lines. You can see them on Google Earth by searching for Nasca Lines.

Decorate the outside to make your instrument bright and colorful. Play it by turning it vertically and allowing the beans to strike the nails inside.

😊 😊 EXPLORATION: Feather Headdresses

Feathers have been worn in South America at initiations and other ceremonies, at funerals, by shamans, to express group identity, to mark life stages, to celebrate holidays, or to exercise political power. Feathers are used partly because they are so beautiful, but also because birds are regarded as sacred by many South American peoples; they are like mediators between people and the gods.

Feathers are also often seen as a sign of a successful hunter and provider, and by extension, as a sign of leadership. Often it is only on initiation into adulthood that a youth is entitled to wear an impressive feather headdress.

You can make feather headdresses using imitation feathers or turkey tail feathers from a craft store. Glue them to a triangular base cut from poster board. Attach the headdress to the child's head by stringing twine through holes in the poster board base.

😊 😊 EXPLORATION: Nasca Lines

As discussed in one history exploration in this unit, the Nasca people made giant outlines of animals and shapes that span the desert of Peru. The Nasca peoples created the huge outlines by scraping away several centimeters of the rock surface to reveal a lighter rock underneath.

There are pictures of several animals – lizards, monkeys, spiders, and also lots of geometric designs. They would have taken years to create, and no one is really certain of their purpose. They are so large that they really aren't very noticeable from the ground at all. They were discovered from surrounding foothills, but they are best seen by flying over them in an airplane.

Historians and archaeologists are really concerned about preserving them because they are actually very shallow carvings that would easily be washed away by rain. It's an area that gets very little rain at all, but it wouldn't take much to destroy the giant works of art. Still, they have already survived many centuries.

The mystery of why these lines were carved is intriguing. Some have theorized that they are star maps and had astrological purposes. Some think they were giant pictures that were gifts to the gods. Some believe they were pleas to the gods for rain. Some have even said the Nasca people made crude hot air balloons to view the art from the air. The theories abound, but we really don't have answers.

Use glue to draw a design on a piece of cardboard. Sprinkle sand over the glue to create your own line picture. Think about some reasons the Nazca people may have created these giant works of art, and share your ideas.

Teaching Tip

Thinking about and discussing art can be just as important to an art unit as actually doing art projects. Try to combine hands on with discussion for the most effective teaching.

Additional Layer

South American art has many of the same animal and nature themes as African art, but with many more colors. Most likely because of the desert environment, African art has many brown hues. South American art, with it's tropical surroundings, has always been full of rich, colorful hues.

Coming up next . . .

My Ideas For This Unit:

Title: ______________________ Topic: ______________________

Title: ______________________ Topic: ______________________

Title: ______________________ Topic: ______________________

My Ideas For This Unit:

Title: ______________________ Topic: ______________________

Title: ______________________ Topic: ______________________

Title: ______________________ Topic: ______________________

Chavin Eagle

This eagle was carved in stone in the cornice of a building from the Chavin culture. It was discovered in 1958. The archaeologists found many other animal carvings as well. Many people have the idea that the ancient South American people were primitive compared with other civilizations of their time, but archaeological evidence shows us that they were actually advanced. Many lived in thriving cities.

Ancient South American Civilizations

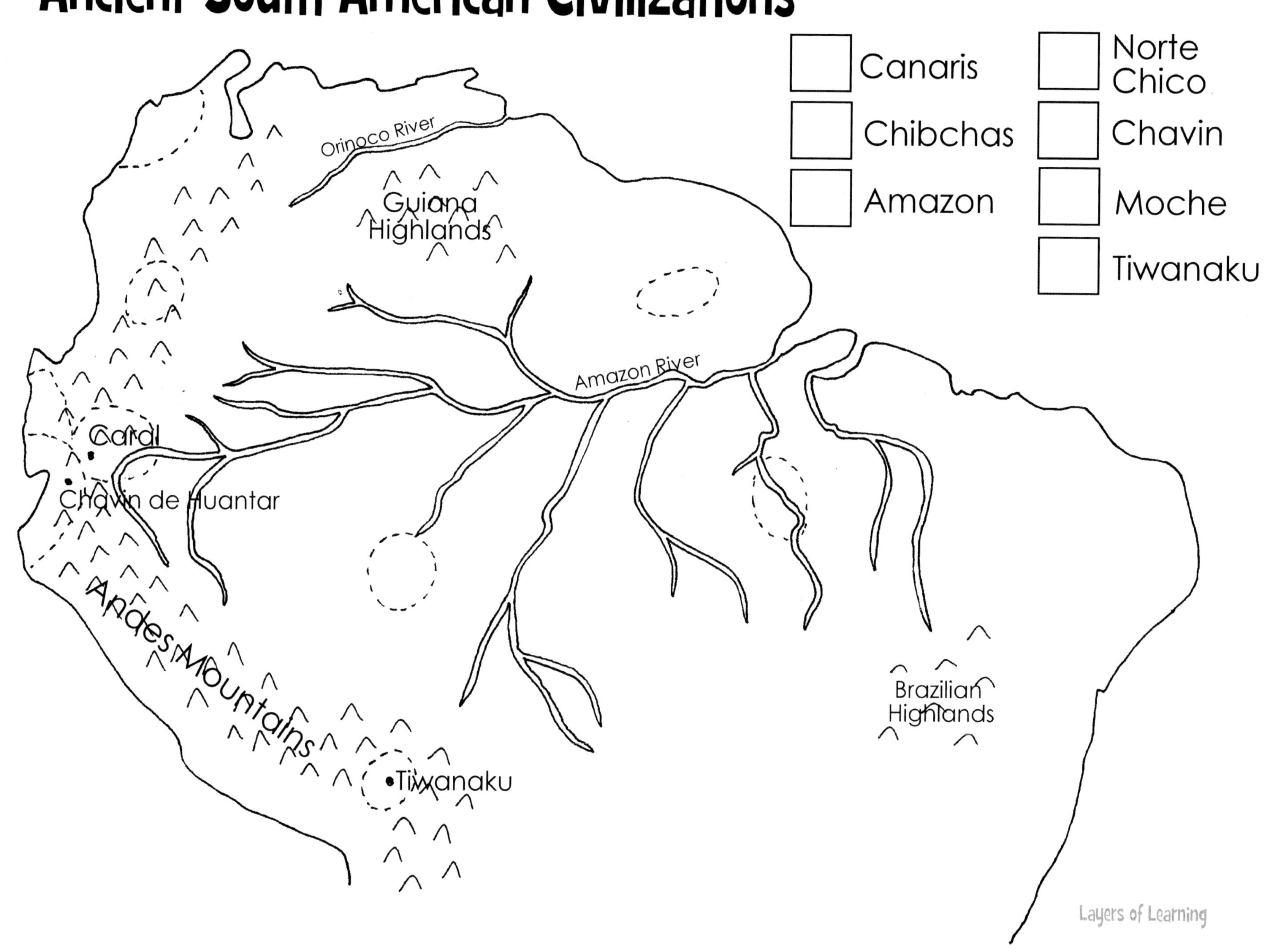

Ancient South America: Unit 1-16

2600-2000 BC 1-16	900 – 200 BC 1-16	400 BC – 1200 AD 1-16	100 – 800 AD 1-16
 Norte Chico civilization at its height	 Chavin civilization *image courtesy of Walters Art Museum*	 Tiwanaku civilization	 Moche civilization

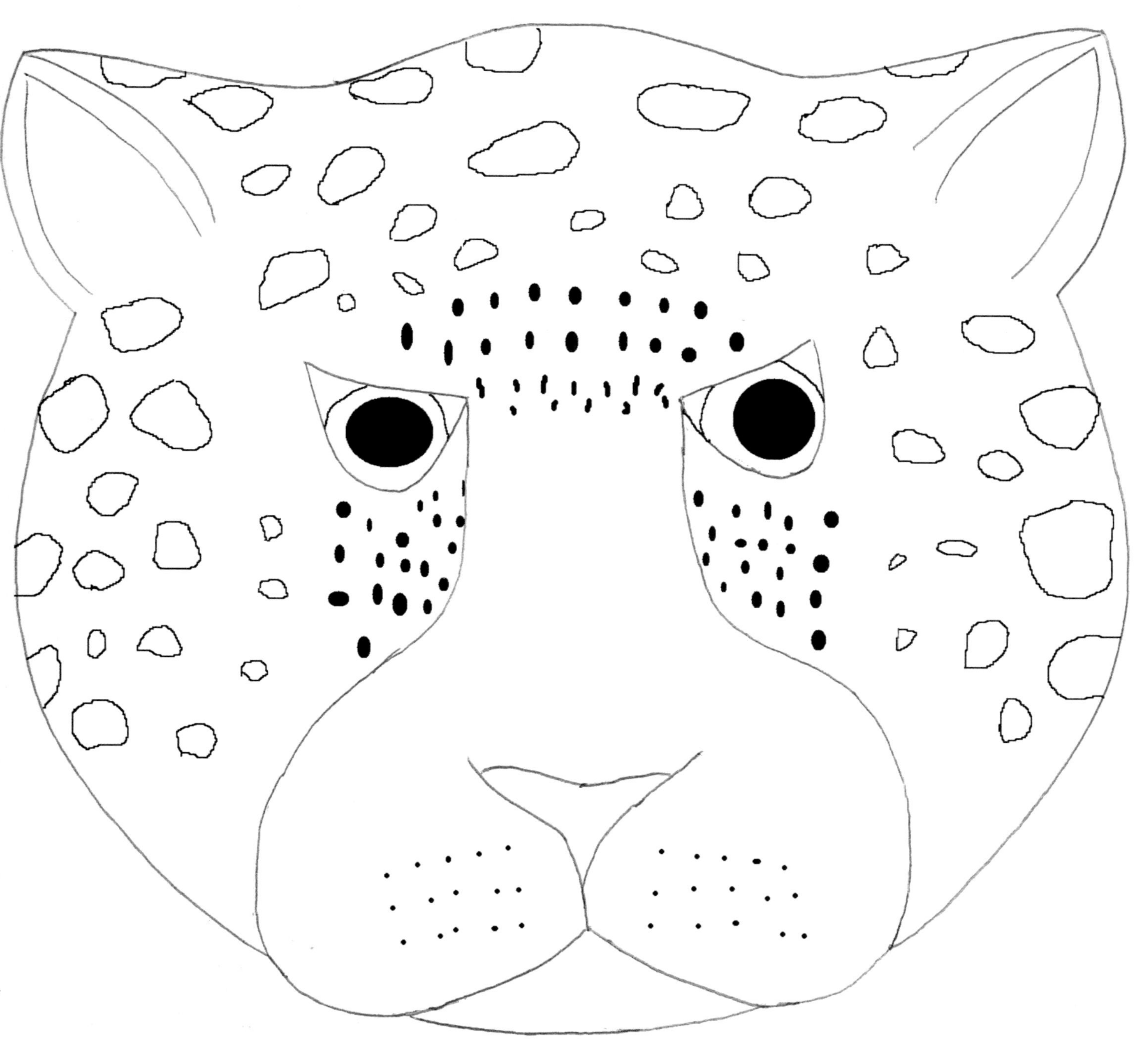

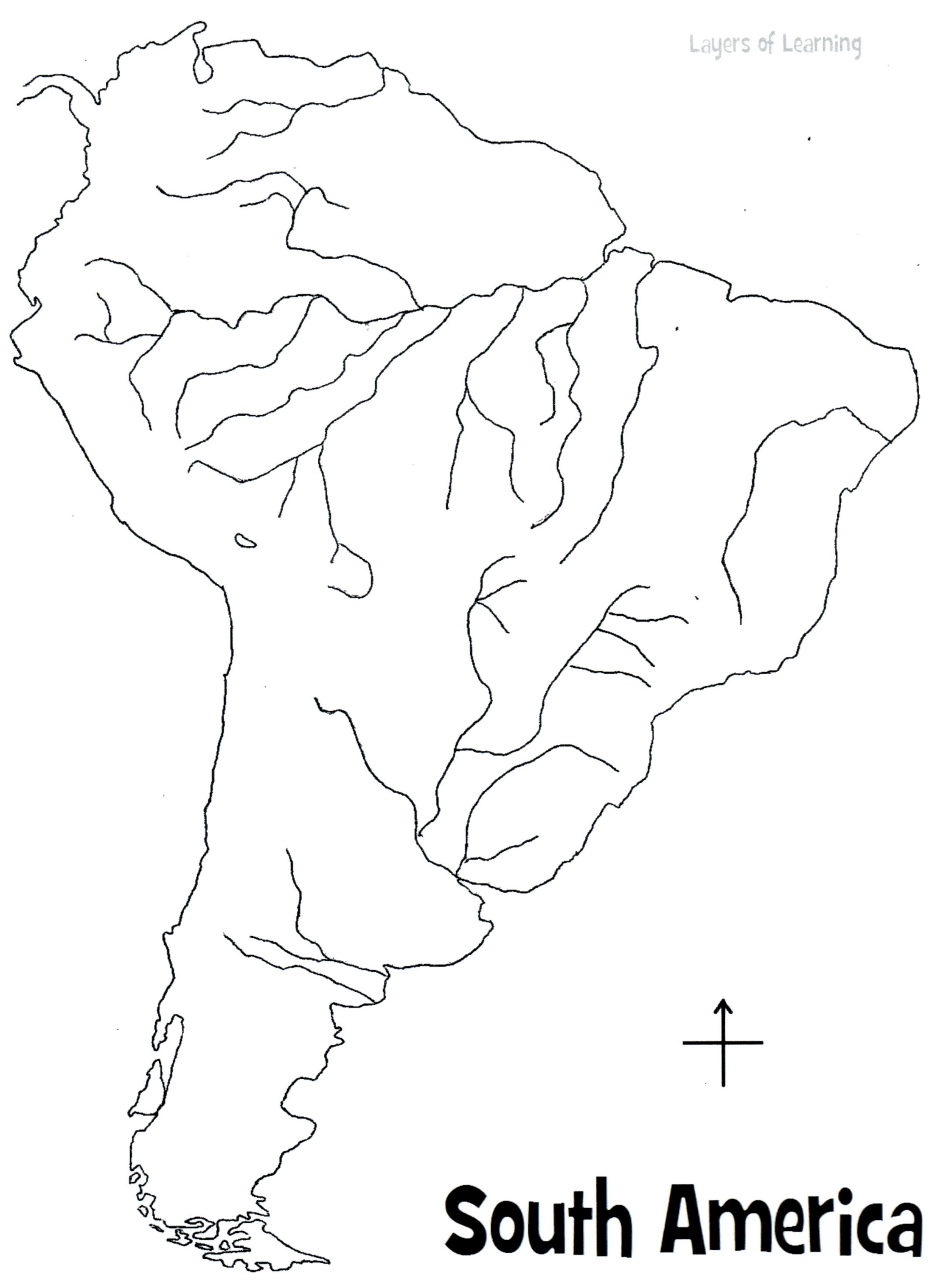
Layers of Learning
South America

South America
Layers of Learning

Draw animals you would find in the Amazon rain forest.

About the Authors

Karen & Michelle . . .
Mothers, sisters, teachers, women who are passionate about educating kids.
We are dedicated to lifelong learning.

Karen, a mother of four, who has homeschooled her kids for more than eight years with her husband, Bob, has a bachelor's degree in child development with an emphasis in education. She lives in Utah where she gardens, teaches piano, and plays an excruciating number of board games with her kids. Karen is our resident Arts expert and English guru {most necessary as Michelle regularly and carelessly mangles the English language and occasionally steps over the bounds of polite society}.

Michelle and her husband, Cameron, homeschooling now for over a decade, teach their six boys on their ten acres in beautiful Idaho country. Michelle earned a bachelor's in biology, making her the resident Science expert, though she is mocked by her friends for being the *Botanist with the Black Thumb of Death*. She also is the go-to for History and Government. She believes in staying up late, hot chocolate, and a no whining policy. We both pitch in on Geography, in case you were wondering, and are on a continual quest for knowledge.

Visit our constantly updated blog for tons of free ideas, free printables, and more cool stuff for sale:
www.Layers-of-Learning.com

Made in the USA
Columbia, SC
04 May 2021

37117628R00029